YEAR OF THE DOG

YEAR OF THE DOG

POEMS

DEBORAH PAREDEZ

A BLESSING THE BOATS SELECTION

AMERICAN POETS CONTINUUM SERIES, NO. 178

BOA EDITIONS, LTD. ◈ ROCHESTER, NY ◈ 2020

First Edition
20 21 22 23 7 6 5 4 3 2 1

For information about permission to reuse any material from this book, please contact The Permissions Company at www.permissionscompany.com or e-mail permdude@gmail.com.

Publications by BOA Editions, Ltd.—a not-for-profit corporation under section 501 (c) (3) of the United States Internal Revenue Code—are made possible with funds from a variety of sources, including public funds from the Literature Program of the National Endowment for the Arts; the New York State Council on the Arts, a state agency; and the County of Monroe, NY. Private funding sources include the Max and Marian Farash Charitable Foundation; the Mary S. Mulligan Charitable Trust; the Rochester Area Community Foundation; the Ames-Amzalak Memorial Trust in memory of Henry Ames, Semon Amzalak, and Dan Amzalak; the LGBT Fund of Greater Rochester; and contributions from many individuals nationwide. See Colophon on page 128 for special individual acknowledgments.

Cover Design: Sandy Knight
Cover Imagery: Photography by Gilberto Villarrcal; "Despair of Hecuba" by Pierre Peyron, The Met
    Collection Rogers Fund, 1965
Interior Design and Composition: Richard Foerster
BOA Logo: Mirko

BOA Editions books are available electronically through BookShare, an online distributor offering Large-Print, Braille, Multimedia Audio Book, and Dyslexic formats, as well as through e-readers that feature text to speech capabilities.

Library of Congress Cataloging-in-Publication Data

Names: Paredez, Deborah, 1970– author.
Title: Year of the dog : poems / Deborah Paredez.
Description: First Edition. | Rochester, NY : BOA Editions, Ltd., 2020. |
  Series: American poets continuum series ; no. 178 | "A Blessing the Boats selection." | Summary: "A
  Latina feminist chronicle of the Vietnam War era in documentary poems that highlights the voices of
  women relegated to the margins of history"— Provided by publisher.
Identifiers: LCCN 2019050299 (print) | LCCN 2019050300 (ebook) | ISBN
  9781950774012 (paperback) | ISBN 9781950774029 (epub)
Subjects: LCGFT: Poetry.
Classification: LCC PS3566.A637 Y43 2020 (print) | LCC PS3566.A637
  (ebook) | DDC 811/.54--dc23
LC record available at https://lccn.loc.gov/2019050299
LC ebook record available at https://lccn.loc.gov/2019050300

BOA Editions, Ltd.
250 North Goodman Street, Suite 306
Rochester, NY 14607
www.boaeditions.org
A. Poulin, Jr., Founder (1938–1996)

For a long time Hecuba remembered
the ancient evils she had undergone
and still continued howling mournfully
through all the fields of Thrace.

—Ovid, *Metamorphoses* (13: 564–72), trans. Ian Johnston

. . . but from here on, I want more crazy mourning, more howl, more keening

—Adrienne Rich, "A Woman Dead in Her Forties"

We are the wrong people of
the wrong skin on the wrong continent and what
in the hell is everybody being reasonable about?

—June Jordan, "Poem about My Rights"

for my parents, Gilberto & Consuelo Villarreal

and for Julie Bathke

CONTENTS

I.

II.

III.

I.

WIFE'S DISASTER MANUAL

When the forsaken city starts to burn,
after the men and children have fled,
stand still, silent as prey, and slowly turn

back. Behold the curse. Stay and mourn
the collapsing doorways, the unbroken bread
in the forsaken city starting to burn.

Don't flinch. Don't join in.
Resist the righteous scurry and instead
stand still, silent as prey. Slowly turn

your thoughts away from escape: the iron
gates unlatched, the responsibilities shed.
When the forsaken city starts to burn,

surrender to your calling, show concern
for those who remain. Come to a dead
standstill. Silent as prey, slowly turn

into something essential. Learn
the names of the fallen. Refuse to run ahead
when the forsaken city starts to burn.
Stand still and silent. Pray. Return.

SELF-PORTRAIT IN THE YEAR OF THE DOG

San Antonio, TX, December 1970

It's nearing the end
of the year and the woman who will be
my mother is pushing
stickpins through the eyes
of sequins and into styrofoam globes
until each coated orb ornaments
the tinseled tree. Her body
is full of the curled question
mark that will soon be
my body. The woman who will be
my grandmother is biding time
at the five and dime stockpiling
supplies to fill my mother's idle
hands. All along she's carried
me low—
         how I've known
from early on to position myself
for descent. When I enter
this world, I'll enter as Hecuba
nearing her end: purpled
and yelping griefbeast,
my mother's spangled
handiwork.

A SHOW OF HANDS

my father taught me never to show
my hand always play the hand
you're dealt don't
bite the hand that feeds you gotta
hand it to him he lived
his life hand to mouth
even before 'Nam he knew
close only counts in
horseshoes and
hand grenades go hand-
to-hand combat idle
hands are the Devil's play
into the enemy's hand it
over and out
of his hands
wringing a bird
in hand is worth two
in the bush he wasn't so good
with his hands took his life
into his own blood
on his hands on the one hand
and on the other

Here is another shot

so you can imagine

LIGHTENING

Chicago, IL, 4 December 1969
for Deborah Johnson (Akua Njeri)

you didn't look

down or back, spent

the fractured minutes

studying each crease

and curve of the law-

men's faces

so later you could tell

    how it happened:

how you crossed over

    his body, how you kept

your hands up

how you didn't

reach for anything

not your opened robe—

nothing—how they said he's good

    and dead

how you crossed

over the threshold

how you lifted one

and then the other

slippered foot across the ice

    how you kept yourself

from falling—how

your bared belly bore

the revolver's burrowing snout—

    how
how

—how when the baby starts

    to descend, it's called

lightening though

it feels like a weight

you cannot bear—lightening

    is when you know

it won't be

long before it's over

YEAR OF THE DOG: SYNONYMS FOR APERTURE

Kent State University, 4 May 1970

Mary Ann Vecchio is down

on her knees. Jeffrey Miller's body is face down

beside her. John Filo presses his finger down

and the aperture shudders. There are four down

when the shooting stops. Mary Ann's arms are out-

stretched, a stripped mast. John is running out

of film. Snowy blossoms shroud the dogwoods out-

side the frame. *This girl came up and knelt over the body and let out*

a God-awful scream, John will say, *that made me*

click the camera. Mary Ann is a 14-year-old runaway. Later she'll say, *I*

hitchhiked my way into history. And later, *It really destroyed my*

life. There will be a song about four dead in Ohio, *O—H—I—*

O—I—OH—OH—OH— The bullet enters Jeffery's opened mouth

and comes out the other side. Mary Ann's mouth

is open, an obliterated star. Synonyms for aperture: mouth—

gap—cleft—chasm—hole—rupture—perforated passage—eye.

In Spanish images of the pietà, the Virgin often holds out one hand

or the other. Mary Ann will get hate mail: *Mary, you*

dirty tramp. It's too bad it wasn't you

that was shot. Or another: *You hippie communist bitch! Did you enjoy sleeping with all those dope fiends and negroes when you were in Ohio?* Mary Ann's mother will say, *Can you imagine her looking at that?*

As her

          open mouth

                      shaped

itself

              for words,

                  trying to

speak,   *she*

              barked.

                  [text: Ovid, *Metamorphoses*]

SELF-PORTRAIT IN FLESH AND STONE

Before the war, my father slid shoehorns between the lips of discount loafers and socked heels.

If the shoe fits, so the story goes, the true identity of the cinder-shrouded girl is known.

Persephone swallowed the seeds and her mother bent fallowed.

My father's mother had nine mouths to feed, ten if she counted herself.

Cronus ate his first five kids and then a stone.

The memorial is cut from polished black granite and cuts into the earth.

My father's name is not cut into the stone but still I see my reflection in its surface.

I tell you, it says in the Book of Luke, *if these remain silent, the stones would cry out.*

My father used to have a mouth on him, but now he reads the Bible and doesn't cuss.

Soldiers in the trenches passed the time sucking on cigarettes and the occasional fruitcake from home until their mouths clouded with rot and they called this trench mouth.

The 56th Dental Detachment, Phu Bai Dental Clinic, was the name of my father's unit.

A dentist once said to Gloria Anzaldúa, *We're going to have to do something about your tongue.*

I inherited my father's gutter mouth, which is not the same as trench mouth.

Soldiers dug 25,000 miles of trenches along the Western Front.

The Viet Cong required North Vietnamese villagers to dig three feet of the Cu Chi Tunnels each day, and this is where they burrowed to escape the bombs bursting in air.

I once pulled myself out of a depression by swallowing herbs and walking each day down the thin slit that cut across the winter-stripped field.

Persephone pulled the narcissus from its root and the dark mouth sucked her down.

There is a photo of my father pulling a rotten tooth from the mouth of a Vietnamese boy.

The trenches would flood and the soldiers would stand for long stretches in the muck unable to remove their wet socks and boots and their feet would soften to rot and they called this trench foot.

I put my foot in my mouth nearly everyday.

Gloria Anzaldúa asks questions that are really refusals, *How do you tame a wild tongue, how do you bridle and saddle it? How do you make it lie down?*

In a 1969 photograph by Horst Faas, a young South Vietnamese woman covers her opened mouth as she stares into a mass grave where she fears her father's body lies.

Many mammals will eat the placenta of their newborns, but some Mexican women I know bury theirs near the hearth.

In 1967, Dang Thi Lanh sang and danced and cooked and crawled and dug with a short hoe and gave birth to her daughter in the Cu Chi Tunnels.

Cronus devoured his children and still his son came back and cast him down.

The soldiers would hump through the monsoon-soaked marsh until their feet bloomed with jungle rot.

My body and my father's body and Plath's body, *Head-stone quiet, jostled by nothing / Only the mouth-hole piped out, / Importunate cricket // In a quarry of silences.*

That time I put my foot in my mouth and asked my father what it was like over there.

My father has never eaten a pomegranate though he has spent time on the other side and its shadow darkens his return.

A mama bird will chew the worm and partially digest it before spitting it out into the mouth of her young and in this way the baby bird is fed.

My father in Phu Bai fingering the dark.

I am surprised sometimes by what comes out of my mouth, so I have to watch my tongue.

Those nights I watched my father's mouth when he dozed off in the recliner to make sure he didn't choke on his tongue during his nightly seizures.

Sometimes the rot was so far advanced they had to amputate the foot to save the man.

I try to swallow the truth but still, like Cronus, it comes out of my mouth anyway.

Yusef Komunyakaa returned from Vietnam and visited the memorial and wrote, *I'm stone. I'm flesh.*

As a defensive strategy, trenches followed a zigzag pattern and never a straight line.

Back home my father slips a hand under the lifted tongue and buffs the black leather until it shines with his reflection, and this is how he meets each week, emptied shoes laid out.

ARMATURE

a call
two arms
akimbo *Arms and*
the gentlemen at arms
length armed to
the teeth arm candy armed
struggle with open arms
inspection give my
right arm strong-arm
bear arms babe
in arms take up
arms shot *In the Arms*
of an Angel up
in arms up arms
up arms up arm-in-
arm twisting
my arm *A Farewell*
to brothers
in arms *These Arms*
of one-
armed bandit with one
arm tied
behind my back the long arm of the law
costs an arm and a leg

YEAR OF THE DOG: AFTER-MATH

Jackson State College, 14–15 May 1970

For as long as folks can
remember the campus
has been split by Lynch
Street, the four-lane thorough-
fare leading back
to town. The stoplights flashing
red at the intersection of Lynch
and any street it meets
making it so
townsfolk can idle and rev
their engines cussing the dark
students trying to cross.

It's not long before the National
Guardsmen march down, before the city
police march up, before the students
hear *We're gonna kill
some o' you nig*—before the thrum
and bleat that follows—

Some students crouch
under dorm room desks.
Some students are running away.
Some students stand still.
Some students are falling down.
Some students climb the stairs.
Some students are screaming.
Some students make no sound.
Some students stay inside.
Some students are bleeding out.

Some students are bowing their heads
over equations, finding the value

of each variable, drawing lines that intersect
in the shape of a cross or an X—

If   100   Students peaceably gathered
If   647   National Guardsmen on duty in Jackson, Mississippi
If   40   Highway Patrolmen
If   27   City Police
If   >200   Rounds fired
If   460   Buckshots fired
If   28   Seconds of gunfire
If   140   Bullet marks on Alexander Women's Dormitory
If   24   Windows into which shots are fired
If   18   Metal panels pocked with buckshot
If   1   Wine bottle dropped from a dormitory window
If   0   Shots fired from inside the dormitory
If   0   Windows left unshattered by gunfire

Then   17   Year-old James Earl Green is dead
Then   21   Year-old Phillip Lafayette Gibbs is dead
Then   12   More students hospitalized
Then   1   Photograph of the shattered façade
Then   1   Bullet-branded, knotted-twisted white
                    curtain still hanging on
Then   2   Dark faces of the risen
                    women looking out of the pane-
                    emptied frame

EDGEWOOD ELEGY

The Edgewood Independent School District, located in a predominantly lower-income Mexican immigrant and Mexican-American west side neighborhood of San Antonio, suffered 54 casualties during the Vietnam War, one of the highest rates for a single school district in the country. My father grew up and attended school in this neighborhood.

I.
Arthur Adame
22 May 1970
Multiple
Frag-   ta/tion
men-
few
Flaco

II.
Adolfo Aguilar, Jr.
14 March 1968
We few

Small Arms
Fire / Body

III.
Enrique Bernal
7 March 1968
La Crotcha (The Corps)

Purple Hearts
Hostile / Ground
Henry

IV.
Gilberto Caballero
6 July 1967

Artillery
we happy
Mortar

V.
Fernando Camarillo
29 May 1968
Other
Explosive

Descansa

V.
my father's documents:
Gilberto C. Villarreal
May 1968
Certificate of Natural—
ization
April 1969
Order
To Report For Induction

VI.
Refugio José Cantú
5 March 1967
Sergeant
Body

En Paz

VII.
Daniel Cardenas

then
shall

our names

VIII.
Rudy Cardenas
26 May 1968
these

In
Country

IX.
Horacio Carranza
2 March 1968
Other

Explosive
patria
mori

X.
Louis Castillo

wounds
Horace

XI.
Ernesto F. Castro
6 August 1968
Drowned
No   Suff-   o   -cated

I had
Airborne

myfather'sdocuments
myfather'sdocuments
myfather'sdocuments
myfather'**s**documents
myfather'**s**documents
myfather'sdocuments
myfather'sdocuments
myfather'**s**documents

XVIII.
Jose Escamilla
10 February 1966

At every
jolt, the blood

XXII.
Estrada Ramon Flores
7 October 1968

Infantry
Div-
Daughter
ision

XIV.
Virgil G. Cruz
28 September 1965

Semper

Other   Accident

XVII.
Christopher G. Delgado
17 February 1968
TET

Lunar Year
Mortar

Monkey

XXI.
Juan Santos

this blood

XIII.
Roy Cisneros
11 September 1968
Navy
disregarding
his own
safety
Cross

XVI.
Mario O. De Leon
20 May 1967
men-

Infantry
Division

XX.
Felix Esparza, Jr.
17 May 1966

mori

XII.
Robert G. Cevallos
12 May 1969

band of
Married
brothers

XV.
Jesus H. De Leon
14 March 1970
Frag-

Brigade

men-

XIX.
Julian Escobedo
1 September 1969
Mission / Hel-
Icopter
A Shau Valley

/body/not—

XXIII.
Rudy Garcia

[Re] Member

XXIV.
Jose Garza, Jr.
18 May 1969

Sergeant
Operation

En Paz

XXV.
Basilio Gomez
18 June 1968
I was

a year old
then

With love,
Basilio Gomez, Jr.

XXVI.
Roy Gonzales, Jr.
5 March 1966

Few

XXVII.
Santiago R. Gonzales
27 February 1967
Selective
Bronze
Star
Service
Jimmy

XXVIII.
Hilario H. Guajardo
1 May 1967
Off-
shore
Crash
at sea
not recovered

XXIX.
Jose A. Gutierrez
28 January 1966
Regular

Wish not
one man
more

XXX.
Raul C. Gutierrez
1 May 1967
SeMper

aIr loss

at seA

XXXI.
Enrique Hernandez

O
do not wish
one more

XXXII.
Heriberto Hernandez
5 December 1968
I feel
like I won't be
coming back
Surrounded by / Bronze
shipmates

XXXIII.
Raymond Hernandez
6 October 1968
my brother
Married
primo
Light In-   fan
try Brig-   ade

brown   man:
carnal *'mano vato*
one   in   two
in   combat
one   in   three
w o u n ded   one
in   five   killed
in   action one

XXXIV.
Robert Litterio
4 September 1968
Identical
Fragment-
Twin
Shadow reflection
of my brother

XXXV.
Joe G. Longoria
19 April 1968
Other
Explosive
Shall be

Baby brother

XXXVI.
Richard Ventura Lopez
24 July 1967
Other
Explosive
my brother
we in it

XXXVII.
Ricardo C. Mendiola
31 January 1970
Other
Explosive
one more

Boyfriend

XXXVIII.
Domingo F. Morado
13 May 1969
Mortar
Morado / Purple
Domingo / Sunday

Tio Mingo

XXXIX.
Robert D. Murphy, Jr.
26 February 1968
Shot through
Heart
Bruthah
Radio

XL.
Armando Navarro
28 August 1968
Division

I answered
I am here
Send me

XLI.
Gilbert Palacios
6 May 1969
Scout Dog
Handler

Walked the line
Man's Best

XLII.
Ramiro R. Ramirez
24 January 1968

Died
while missing

band of

XLIII.
Tommy Rendon
29 March 1968
His blood

we few

brothers

INDUCTION
you are here—
by   ordered
bring   enough
clean   clothes
for three days
bring   enough
money   to last

XLIV.
Joe M. Riojas

dulce

XLV.
Fidencio G. Rios
6 July 1970

Other
de

XLVI.
Jesus M. Robledo, Jr.
21 August 1968
Grunt
Platoon
Hell Bro
ke

XLVII.
Raul Ruiz, Jr.

Bro
thers
-corum

XLVIII.
Fermin Saldaña, Jr.
23 May 1966

Letter home:
Someone
has
to do it.

NATURALIZ—
ation-**ation**-ation
Intends to reside
Per man- ently
In the United
States / entitled
in all
Other respects

XLIX.
Gregorio Valdez III
30 January 1966
His
Pistol

In His / Small
Arms / *Hand* / Fire

L.
̄ **Juan Vallin**

jolt

LI.
Gregory J. Van de Walle
14 May 1967
then
Purple
Body
let him
let him

LII.
Edward Vela, Jr.

our names

–No–

LIII.
Jimmy Lee Woolfolk
19 December 1967
Air / Loss

4 December 1967

Crash / Land

LIV.
Armando M. Zepeda
22 May 1971

depart

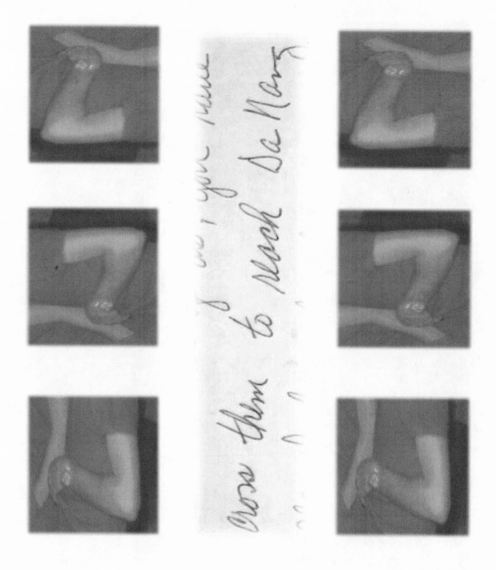

HEARTS AND MINDS

So, we must be ready to fight in Vietnam, but the ultimate victory will depend upon the hearts and minds of the people who actually live out there.
—Lyndon Johnson, 1965

don't lose [   ]
bear in [   ]

cross your [   ] hope
to die / a legend

in your own [   ] / bleeding [   ]
presence of [   ] / your absence made

[   ] grow fonder
change your [   ] / strike

fear in the [   ] / call
to [   ] / hand over

your [   ] / peace
of [   ] / home

is where the [   ]
is / stuck in

your [   ] / your [   ] not
in it / nothing could be

further from
your [   ]

SELF-PORTRAIT IN ONE ACT

DRAMATIS PERSONAE:

EVERETT ALVAREZ, falls from the sky and breaks the surface of the gulf, first American aviator POW captured in Vietnam, brother to Delia

DELIA ALVAREZ, cast in the role of dutiful, patriotic, mourning sister but keeps breaking character

NARRATOR, sister and daughter and poet who prefers theatre that breaks the fourth wall

NARRATOR'S BROTHER, breaks his femur on the playing field

NARRATOR'S FATHER, breaks in his combat boots

ANTIGONE, breaks with the state and buries her brother

FRANKIE GAYE, breaks the airwaves with his voice as an Army radio-telephone operator (RTO), breaks the news about the war in letters home to his brother, Marvin

MARVIN GAYE, breaks out in song

POET-CHORUS, breaks into soliloquies by Lucille Clifton, Stanley Kunitz, and Adrienne Rich

SCENE 1: A GULF
Enter EVERETT, shot down from the flak-blackened August sky into the Gulf of Tonkin. When his captors pull him from the water, his first response is to break into Spanish.

EVERETT: *Don't ask me why I did that. It seemed like a good idea.*

Enter NARRATOR, FRANKIE, DELIA, and POET-CHORUS across the gulf.

NARRATOR: Theatre teaches me to speak out in superstitious code, as in
                   "The Scottish Play" or "Break a Leg!"

FRANKIE: The Army teaches me to speak out in code, like when you want to get through with your emergency message and there's too much radio traffic, you say, "BREAK, BREAK."

POET-CHORUS: *In a murderous time / the heart breaks and breaks / and lives by breaking.*

NARRATOR: In Spanish, the word for brotherhood is hermanidad. The word for sisterhood is hermanidad. It's the same word.

DELIA: *The mentality that calls Vietnamese 'gooks' is the same mentality that calls brown people 'spics.' It's the same battle.*

SCENE 2: A CLEARING
Enter FRANKIE and NARRATOR carrying the body of the NARRATOR'S BROTHER who has broken his femur on the playing field.

Enter ANTIGONE, falling from her nest with a broken wing, nestling in near the NARRATOR'S BROTHER.

ANTIGONE: I am daughter and sister to Oedipus, and my name means "in place of one's parents."

NARRATOR: Unlike my brother, I've never broken a bone but I have broken my word.

FRANKIE: The RTO alphabet teaches me another way to spell the words I know.

ANTIGONE: I confess to knowing the word of the law and breaking it anyway.

FRANKIE: Bravo Romeo Oscar Tango Hotel Echo Romeo OVER

Enter Marvin and Delia, en hermanidad.

MARVIN: *What's going on?*

DELIA:	I have learned another way to spell "Tonkin:" T / On / Kin.
NARRATOR:	My brother is young and spared.
DELIA:	*The war went beyond just my brother.*
MARVIN:	*Picket lines (sister), Picket signs (sister)*
NARRATOR:	My brother's spare parts.
FRANKIE:	Sierra India Sierra Tango Echo Romeo OVER
DELIA:	COPY
FRANKIE:	Sierra India Sierra Tango Echo Romeo OVER
MARVIN:	*What's happening, brother? What's happening, brother?*
NARRATOR'S BROTHER:	My part is spare.
FRANKIE:	OUT

Exit FRANKIE carrying NARRATOR'S BROTHER on his back.

Sound of radio static.

NARRATOR:	Sticks and stones may break my bones, but words will always cleave me.
ANTIGONE:	I told my sister I had no use for her words. I'd done the deed, breaking open the earth and gathering the sticks and stones to cover our brother's grave.

Sound of dead air.

Enter POET-CHORUS, breaking the silence.

POET-CHORUS:	*break, October, speak, / …thrust / your tongue against mine, break / day*

NARRATOR: I hang blackout curtains in the bedroom, which makes it hard to see daybreak.

SCENE 3: THE HOMEWRECK

Enter NARRATOR'S FATHER in civilian clothes and EVERETT, returning after eight years of captivity. They begin to slow dance together following the rhythm of a reporter's voice over the radiowaves.

VOICE OF
REPORTER: *Just before you came home, your sister, Delia, said, "All hell might break loose" when you find out about her antiwar activity. What happened when you did find out about it?*

Enter NARRATOR, DELIA, and POET-CHORUS, out of time.

NARRATOR: In "The Scottish Play," the king and queen cannot rid themselves of the blood on their hands.

POET-CHORUS: *It is all blood and breaking, / blood and breaking*

NARRATOR: My father was young and spared.

EVERETT: *Well, first of all, all hell did not break loose.*

NARRATOR'S
FATHER: I came home in time to escort my sister to her senior prom.

EVERETT and NARRATOR'S FATHER dance together offstage.

Enter DELIA who begins a slow dance with NARRATOR to the sounds of MARVIN's song, "What's Going On?"

DELIA: *Everett will return when Vietnamese children will be able to look at the sky and clouds—*

NARRATOR: If the breaking of character is particularly serious, it is called "corpsing."

DELIA: *and not fear that a bomb will drop that will burn and tear their bodies—*

The sound of Marvin's voice rises as the women continue their dirge-dance.

MARVIN voice: *Brother brother brother, there's far too many of you dying.*

FIN

MOTHER TONGUE

If I could, I'd grow tongues in my arms and hands
and hair, in the soles of my feet—a thousand tongues
all talking, all crying together . . .
    —Hecuba in Euripides' *Hecuba*

If I could bite my tongue
and have it split into two
whole daughters that split
again in endless fission-
ing, splitting the very thing
keeping their whole line
going—If I could I would
watch my tongue and its
tongue-set wagging
their tails, some silver-
tongued, some wicked—
I'd hold my tongue
out like an offering or
a battalion, a thousand
tongues talking in their
native tongue, a forked-
tongue language, all
of them speaking
in tongues and tongue-
lashing like Medusa's head
or the tentacles of a giant
squid—I'd stick out
all of my tongues—I'd let
my tongues loose
and lassoing my
prey—some slither-
whipped, some wick-
snuffed—I'd leave them
all—*wild tongues can't be*
tongue- *tamed they can*
only be—tied—*cut*—

YEAR OF THE DOG: A ROCK AND A HARD PLACE

Alcatraz Island & Petaluma, CA, Summer 1970

STATION *v.* **1.** To assign a post, position, or place to a person: As when my father is stationed at an infirmary in Petaluma the year before he's stationed at the 56th Dental Detachment in Phu Bai, Vietnam. **2.** To position oneself, take up one's (preferred) place: As when the Indians of All Tribes station themselves at Alcatraz Island for 19 months from November 1969 until June 1971.

STATION *n.* **1.** A place or position to which a person is assigned, esp. for duty: As when the first protesters swam ashore and the island's caretaker abandoned his station, crying out over the radio: *Mayday! Mayday! The Indians have landed!* **2.** The place or position occupied by a person or thing: It isn't long after the Indians occupy Alcatraz and proclaim *We hold the Rock!* that my father arrives at the Army Security Agency Field Station in Two Rock Valley, named after a paved-over Indian Trail. This isn't long after the government had closed the prison and the light station on the island and had declared Alcatraz *surplus federal property* in 1963. **3.** A place where a particular kind of business or service is carried out; a base or center equipped for a particular purpose. Frequently with modifying word: Back in 1913, a local newspaper giddily (and erroneously) proclaimed, *Alcatraz Island is to be abandoned as a military prison and converted into the most modern immigration station in America. . . . Those detained would not have to be watched, as there can be no escape from Alcatraz.* **4.** A person's position in life as determined by external circumstances or conditions: Every Indian's station in life is marked by broken treaties like the Treaty of Fort Laramie in 1868, which proclaimed all abandoned federal land should be returned to the Indians who once occupied it. **5.** A band of frequencies used by a particular broadcasting company; a channel: Weekends my father crosses the bridge spanning the bay and tunes the radio to a station playing Joplin's scratchy version of Gershwin's promise, *One of these mornings / You're gonna rise, rise up singing.* Sometimes he sings along, and sometimes he keeps rolling the dial down past the static to a pirated station where Buffy Sainte-Marie is singing *the treaties are broken again and again* and John Trudell is welcoming listeners to *Radio Free Alcatraz from Indian Land Alcatraz Island.* **6.** A place in which a person chooses to position herself; a place or position taken up as a viewpoint: As when LaNada Means takes up her station as a leader in the occupation, staying on for the duration and managing the finances and meeting with lawyers and handling reporters and looking after her children and drafting a grant proposal for a park and an Indian cultural center and school on the island—though it's hard to know all this with the men getting all the credit. **7.** The place in which a thing stands or is positioned; a thing's (proper) location: Graffiti stationed at the island's entrance: *INDIANS WELCOME. UNITED ~~STATES~~ INDIAN PROPERTY.* Cf. **LOCATION**.

LOCATION *n.* **1.** An area or region in which something takes place or is situated; a setting. Frequently with qualifying adjective: Back during World War II, the military base in Petaluma was called Two Rock Station and was an ideal location for intercepting enemy radio communications. By the time my father arrived, they'd changed the name and their tactics and had transformed a corner of the compound into a Vietnamese village for training the troops on-location. **2.** The particular place or position occupied by a person or thing: John Trudell's voice breaks the airwaves: *The question has been asked why did we choose to occupy an abandoned prison rather than a more desirable land location. The answers are many and to we, Indian people, they are obvious. Alcatraz Island is a symbol of what we Indian people have today. It bears a remarkable resemblance to reservation life as neither have enough water, there are no natural resources, and the government cannot find any use for it.* **3.** *Computing.* A position or address in memory: Trudell signals his location over the radio: *Even the rocks which seem to lie dumb as they swelter in the sun thrill with memories of past events connected with the fate of my people.* **4.** An area of land occupied by a particular population group, esp. one set aside for the use of indigenous peoples; a reserve. Now *historical.* Cf. **RELOCATION**

RELOCATION *n.* The act of reallocating something; the action of moving to a new location: Back in 1953, Congress established a policy of *Termination* toward Indians which sounds redundant but which actually meant the end of government support for Indian tribes and protected status for Indian lands and which led to the *Indian Relocation Act of 1956*, which offered Indians a one-way bus ticket from their tribal lands to cities like San Francisco, places where they often found themselves unsettled and unemployed and suffering from a sense of cultural and financial dislocation. Cf. **DISLOCATION**

48

DISLOCATION *n.* **1.** Displacement of a bone from its natural position in the joint: As when my father drives the ambulance from Petaluma across the bridge to the Letterman Army Hospital at the Presidio while the guy in the gurney cries out from the split center of his body, from what the medic calls a posterior dislocation of the hip. **2.** Removal from its proper (or former) place or location: Low on the dial, John Trudell describes the dislocation of his people who *are few and resemble the scattering trees of the storm-swept plain.* **3.** *fig.* The state of being "out of joint" or thrown into confusion or disorder; disarrangement: As when my father arrives at the emergency room and the doctor on duty tells him and the medic to take hold of the guy on the gurney and then proceeds with considerable force to pop the hip back in place, and later, when the guy is up and walking again and he tells my father how he's still got this lingering feeling of dislocation, how once something's out of joint there's no putting it back the way it was before. As in the year to come, when my father and LaNada Means and John Trudell and all the others are forced out, as when relocation orders, as when one-way, as when static on the station, as when years later my father and LaNada and John come home but still feel that lingering sense of dislocation, as when thrown stones sink and settle onto the storm-swept bay floor even as the ripples they've made shirr the surface and reach for shore.

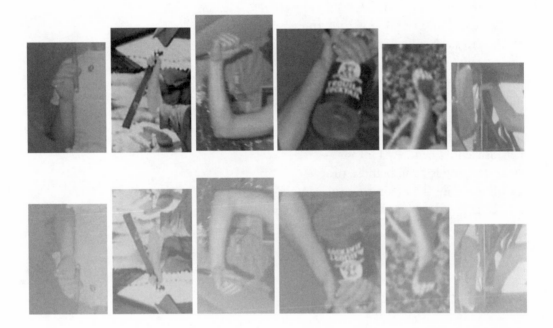

SELF-PORTRAIT WITH WEEPING WOMEN

I know why I fell hard for Hecuba—
shins skinned and lips split to blooming lupine
on her throat's rough coat, *hurled down the whole length*
of disaster—I'm sure I'd grown to know
by then to slacken as a sail against
the current and squall of a woman's woe.
What could I do but chorus my ruddered
howl to hers? When you're a brown girl raised up
near the river, there's always a woman
bereft and bank-wrecked, bloodied and bleating
her insistent lament. Ay Llorona—
every crossing is a tomb and a tune,
a wolf-wail and the moon that turns me to
scratch at the tracks of every mud-dirged girl.

HELEN'S ABOUT FACE

just another pretty
face that launched
a thousand shit-
faced-two-faced
face to face
the facts blowing up
in my face off
the face of the earth blue
in the face of
danger all for what's
his face all up in my long
face down face
forward can't see
the hand in front of my slap
in the face only a mother
could cut off the nose
to spite to save to wipe
that smile off my game face
the music falling flat
on my face
value written all over my
typeface

YEAR OF THE DOG: *SOLEDAD*

New York Women's House of Detention, December 1970
for Angela Davis

though you are their sole suspect

though they capture you on Columbus Day

though their conqueror's pallor dulls the night's obsidian pulse

though they smash the whorled tips of your fingers against the ink

though they single you out beyond a doubt

though they lock you away from the others

though inside these walls *book* is a shackled verb and not a shared noun

though they hand your beaten body over to another state authority

though they make you move through their thicket of rifles

though your cuffed wrists won't let you raise your fists

though your shoulders shiver in your jailhouse shift

though your teeth break the chilled silence with drumroll chatter

though your feet turn snowmelt

though the white drifts will bury others

you will not be kept
solitary for long

you will turn salt-pillar steady
elusive moonpool

you will circulate
your smuggled copy of *Soledad Brother* to your sisters

you will refuse
to shuffle or stumble on your shackled walk

you will say the names of the ones still inside
Helen and *Harriet* and *Vernell* and *Laura* and *Amy* and *Pat* and *Minnie* and *Joann*

you will know there is nothing singular
about you

you will know you are a compound
word like *everybody* or *underground* or *elsewhere* or *blackbird* or *railroad*—

in the place where I'm from *Soledad* is
a word and a sentence

Soledad is the name a woman is given

Soledad is a sentence a woman must serve
for the rest of her life

Soledad is the gavel and the holding pen

Soledad is the person and the state
of being she lives out

Soledad is the letter sent from a locked cell

Soledad is the name we sometimes call
our most holy *Virgen*

Soledad insists on service to it

Soledad is the sentence
you will spend your life writing

II.

On the morning of June 8, 1972, Phan Thi Kim Phúc fled with her family from the Cao Dai Temple near Tráng Bàng during a misdirected napalm attack by South Vietnamese forces. The napalm burned through her clothes, leaving third degree burns on her back and arms. Nick Ut, a South Vietnamese photographer for the AP, photographed her running with others down Route 1 before accompanying her to the hospital. The photograph ran the next morning in papers across the world and is thought to be largely responsible for hastening the end of U.S. involvement in the war. In the years since, Kim Phúc has often been referred to simply as the "Napalm Girl."

KIM PHÚC IN THE TEMPLE OF CAO DAI

Tráng Bàng, June 8, 1972

No place
safe left
save the village
temple or so
you've all been
told: two handfuls
of soldiers, nearly a score
of neighbors killing
time in the lull.

Now the third day
in, the sky flame-
rouged, you are running
after the younger
children: Cousin Danh still
unsteady in his steps
toddling toward the black
bird—flight-awry—now
shuttered indoors now
shuddering now stilled
by the boy's grasp now
the grownups shouting—
No! An omen!—now
the wing-thrashed
release now the ascent.

You reach out
but Danh has fallen
in a fit at the loss
of what he once
held, no matter what
you do, he won't
be consoled.

There she was   *the child*

in her

birdgrief

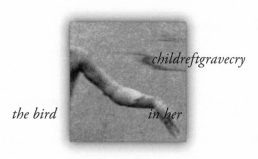

childreftgravecry

the bird   *in her*

howling

and

cursing

[text: Sophokles/Carson, *Antigonick*]

KIM PHÚC IN THE BLAST

Route 1, Tráng Bàng, June 8, 1972

Phosphorus smoke   slithering   into the temple   garden

     target   marking   the falling

Hard bombs drop heavily to the ground, but

         Then I saw the fire everywhere around me

the lighter napalm canisters tumble end over

                 falling face

down   *Actually, I was in the middle*

     of that   end, making forward progress   *I was running*

as they head earthward   *running, running away*

—huh huh   huh huh   huh huh   huh   huh   huhhuhhuhhuhhuhhuhhuuu—

      I tore off   unwritten

        my burning   rule of engagement:

clothes   jellied sleeve of flame   no fire directed at unarmed

     But the burning   Vietnamese unless they were

       didn't   running   runningrurningburning

        stop   Anyone running

       could be assumed   *I was alone*

blackened back neck   brurningbreakneck   ponytorchtail   *to be fleeing Viet*

with that terrible   *Nóng quá*   Cong

Má   *nóng quá*   and therefore fair

heat   game

The highway is very narrow

KIM PHÚC IN THE PHOTOGRAPH

Route 1, Tráng Bàng, June 8, 1972

Frame 1: Nick Ut / Horst Faas

After the black smoke I saw

first, one woman

I keep shooting and shooting

then I saw

                                  It's

the girl

                          a picture

her arm

                                that

just running

                            doesn't

open big

                                rest

mouth

gap—
    cleft—
       chasm—
          hole—
        rupture—
           perf
        orated
          pass
       age—

eye

Frame 2: Eye to Eye

by the time the body's caught
in the camera's eye
the subject turns object—
arms are winged black-
bird's eye view of the
strikes what strikes
the eye is the body
flayed naked the naked
eye can't see the eyes
in back of the back no
skin off the back straw
breaking the camel's eye
of the need the blind
eye of just the scales
falling from the eyes
opened on the opened
morning papers

Frame 3: William Westmoreland

WESTMORELAND SAYS

I said

  HIBACHI

it was told to me

  NOT NAPALM

that she was

  burnedBURNED

by a hi—

  GIRL

dark faces of the risen

women looking out of the

pane—

Frame 4: Kim Phúc / Nhất Chi Mai

The first time I look   *I wish*

at that picture   *to use my body*

I say, Oh   *as a torch*

my goodness!   *to dissipate*

Why he took   *the darkness*

that picture?   *to awaken love*

But later on, I   *among people*

have to accept that—   *and bring*

that picture   *peace to Vietnam.*

Hence

I was trying

       still going forward

picture of the

          napalm

again

[text: Choi, *Hardly War*]

KIM PHÚC IN THE BARSKY BURN UNIT

Saigon, June-November 1972

Nights when the nurses turn back to their stations your father acts as if he's
observing visiting hours as if he's on his way out when really what he's doing is
preparing the body smoothing every fray of himself until he is reed or blade or
thread enough to slip underneath the bed where you lie unconscious face down
he fears you will not make it back from this he cannot leave you he will lie in
wait for your spirit to loosen its springs who else will know to take you back to
be buried with the ancestors who else will know the moment you're gone you
must be taken back to lie among the others so you will not come back to haunt
the family as a restless ghost he's flat on his back blinking against the bed's
underside the patchwork of coils unsprung you make it to morning and he's back
at it fighting back tears as he hears your shattered cries your high whine your low
moan in the burn bath the nurses peeling back the skin that hasn't fastened or
sloughing the grafts swelling with infection your wails the wails of flayed prey
you've left language behind deadened tissues snipped all along your back dabbed
and dressed the days patched and bound into weeks then three months in he sees
your shuttered eyes alive in moth-flicker he knows you're making your way back
to him bowing toward you he whispers *Phúc do you know your father?* he keeps
asking *Phúc do you know your father?* until you answer back one word—*Know*—
the word a hammer strike or a snake's the moment he knows you've come back he
knows you will live *Phúc has come back to herself* he will tell your mother and he
will bring back a split spiny-skinned soursop and together you will eat the fruit
and know there's no turning back now

the back

ground.

KIM PHÚC IN THE SPECIAL PERIOD

Havana, Cuba, Spring 1992

The cane fields, leave-
wisped with their green
secrets. Stalk thickets stay
uncut. The mill machines stilled.

There's no fuel so no
one's going anywhere soon
though many know how
tires not only spin but float.

The sugar can't be processed
by your body is what the doctors
say and prescribe you special
dietary instructions.

You're not alone with your special
needs. Everyone here knows
where there's blood there's sugar
that must be controlled.

You've come to grow used
to *special*. You've come through
enemy fire, your scarred arms
rising now like coppiced cane.

In the countryside, smoke-
stacks loom billowless.
In the city, people wait
in line under a billowless sky.

You've given up
on medicine. Now you're learning
the enemy's language. Nothing
special. Just the everyday

conjugations of your body's verbs:
I burn, I live, I leave,
I burned, I lived, I left,
I will burn, I will live, I will leave

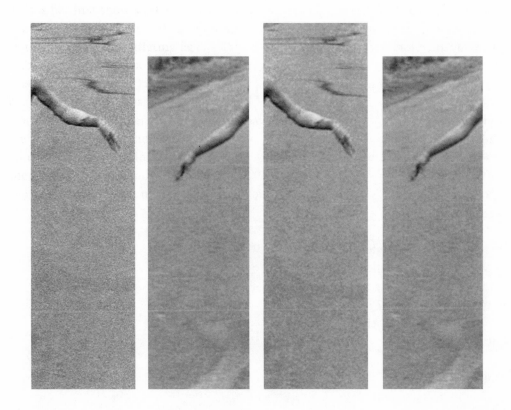

KIM PHÚC IN THE TEMPLE OF THE SUN

Teotihuacán, Mexico, 25 July 1992

Here you are
in the shadows of another
temple, this time the holy place
where my ancestors once
made their offerings,
burning their girl-effigies.

Today's the day
when the sun's supposed
to shine directly over the top
of the pyramid at noon—
a position designed
for perfect alignment.

The pyramids are divided
by what the Aztecs called
Miccaotl, by the passageway
now called *Calzada de los Muertos*—
the dead you cannot help
but cross.

You've come this far
hoping to keep crossing
past the stacked stones
of the vanquished. But your
minders won't let you
out of their sight.

Today's not the day.
There are eyes everywhere
like the scalded milk-wash of the sun.
There's no hiding, so you pose
for a photo against the steps leading nowhere
but closer to the sun's noonday glare.

How are you captured
in this shot? Looking back? Off
in the distance beyond the temple
gates? The sun at your back,
a yoke tethering the body
to the earth it must break.

III.

SELF-PORTRAIT WITH HOWLING WOMAN

My father comes home but not
before he makes a stop in Saigon to drop some cash on a Sanyo reel-to-reel.

Sound is made only when the tape unspools
properly from the supply reel to the take-up reel which must start out empty to do its job.

Mostly he threads the howling sound
of Janis Joplin's scuffed pleas, *please please please please come on come back to me.*

To hear the other side
of the tape slipping through the reel you have to reverse its direction of movement.

A person suffering
from post-traumatic stress is often pulled back to the past through recurring flashbacks.

Some words recur
in Joplin's songs: *please, daddy, honey, maybe, baby, cry, try, come back, come on, no.*

Audio frequency refers
to the range of sound that is audible to the human ear.

When he plays the bellow and squall
of her voice, he turns up the volume until even the neighbors can hear.

Cry cry baby
cry baby cry baby honey welcome back home

A rotating spindle
called a capstan allows the tape to run at a precise and constant speed.

Prolonged Exposure is one
treatment that requires the patient to retrieve and reckon with what they've buried.

A pinch roller
presses against the capstan to provide the friction necessary to pull the tape.

Oh daddy daddy daddy daddy
Try yeah try yeah try yeah oh try try yeah I said try try try try try try try oh try yeah try

A new sound can be recorded
over an old one but once you've taped over the original there's no retrieving it.

Audio stimulation and other external stimuli
like hand tapping or directed eye movement are used on the patient in EMDR treatment.

Any imperfection on the polished surface
of the capstan can cause a flutter or a drag in the motion of the tape.

I keep movin' on but I never find
out why I keep pushin' so hard I keep tryin' to make it right through another lonely day

There's a small amount of drag
left on the supply wheel to maintain the necessary tension for the tape to play smoothly.

Sometimes he cuts the tape
at the angle of a backslash, splicing out the sounds he no longer wants to hear.

Here they are re-building

LAVINIA WRITING IN THE SAND, 1973

Second-hand newlywed bed rocked
by his arched back, gasps for more
air, quickened buckling, then

collapse. This is the first time
his body ricochets
with the crooked electricity,

the first time she sees him
this way, spasm-gripped
as the seizure intercepts his sleep.

Lucky for him, she's fresh
from nursing school, knows
enough to take him into her

arms, still his jaw to keep him
from biting his tongue, turn
his face against the choking.

This is the bed they will make
for me. Evenings will come
when I'll watch him drift off

in the recliner and hear her voice
from the kitchen, *Make sure
your father doesn't swallow*

his tongue. Some
will say it's not possible
to do such a thing, but

I will grow to see the body
flailing dusk after dusk after—
and the whole house gone silent.

Awake!

Awake!

So to speak.

Deborah!   *Awake!*

Awake!

So to speak.

a   *song!*   *utter*

[text: Judges 5:12]

MEMORIAL DAY GHAZAL

—still, Hecuba's howl unchaining her voice,
stations cleaving from the train in her voice.

Engine's low thunder: a thousand cranes strung
and unwinged in the skein of its voice.

The trees are bare and veined with ice and still
The stones of strange fruit remain in her voice.

Desert swallow's morning complaint, the sigh
Of languishing stars made plain in its voice.

Rain shuddering down on Canaan—and Deborah
Mud-struck and worn, war chant straining her voice.

```
your [      ] /  your [       ]
not                 your [      ] / your [      ] not
                    your [     ]
              /  your [     ]
not
```

LAST

The last Huey is lifting off
that Saigon rooftop—
broken line of families, dark
hair aloft in the blades'
wake, and our relay

team is finishing last
at the annual track meet—
girls angled in staggered
lines, bodies half-turned
back toward the ones

approaching. They'll stay
on that roof and no other
chopper will land—hours
like years, climbing
down, backs against

the emptied sky, ochre clouds
of track dust kicked up and
settling. We run. We finish
last, we meet each
others' waiting hands.

keeps me

SURNAME VIET GIVEN NAME NAM

```
                    the women keep                                              ex
ceeding                                                                    the fra
me
                              they         display us in shop windows for for
eign visitors who come to look at our li  ves  as if we were          polite   an        i
mals


hands swaying  praying  waving a                                    flag or fan
                                               sewing   rowing   holding a net or a
                    knife
                                          [in  audible]
                                                                               cut
ting fabric or carrots or setting her     self  trans
on fire
                    [un                        a con
lated passage]                                 ans then media
                                               of the war by other
                    if the war is
tinuation of politics by other me                     [translation and con
images are the continuation                    ve; you see, tú ves]
                    means
                                                    fingers inter
             jugation: I see;   yo
                                               as for my husband, I was left
locked and splayed
                                                          [closeup
without news                                   ear          empty holed

                    of her pierced                Always recurring in
lobe]                                          a time when the witnesses themsel
     the prisoner's mind is the fear of        explosions of life and of death
ves  die without witness, when history         relays
     cons              ists of tiny                       [inaudible]
                    without                    translate
          [inaudible]                          ear?
                    do   you
          by eye or by                         the women's speech is
                                                          tenor and vehicle and not
          the tenor of                         at all
grave              the women are
a metaphor
```

Here we are about half

YEAR OF THE DOG: WALLS AND MIRRORS

Fall 1982

The wall dematerializes as a form and allows the name to become the object . . .
—Maya Lin, designer of the Vietnam Veterans Memorial

The English translation of my surname is *walls*
misspelled, the original *s* turned to its mirrored
twin, the *z* the beginning of the sound for sleep.

I'm nearly twelve and the mirror is a disaster I
learn to turn away from, the girl looking back
always looking to extract her pound of flesh.

I had a simple impulse to cut into the earth,
Maya Lin is writing as the mirrored wall
of names she's made is arranged and laid

against the riven hillside. *I never looked
at the memorial as a wall*, she writes, *but
as an edge to the earth, an opened side.*

For a wall to become a mirror it must not
absorb or scatter too much light; for a girl
to become the protagonist she must sleep

with the guy or until he kisses her awake.
Sometimes we know she's the fairest one
of all because of the mirror on the wall.

Sometimes she must scale the city's walls
to bury the guy. Antigone cuts into the earth
to give him his proper memorial. She ends

up the heroine and buried alive, an *in-be-
tween thing*, like someone who's eleven or
nearly twelve. When I look at the number

11 I see two walls, my name and its mirrored
twin. Sometimes 11 resembles the mirrored
L's at the end of *wall* or the beginning of *llanto*,

the Spanish word for weeping. Sometimes 11
looks like a pair of railway sleepers arranged
and laid along a track that's always leading me

back to my war-worn father. Sometimes the guy
comes back from battle and has seizures
in his sleep and the girl must shake him awake.

Sometimes the wall and the name are one
and the same. Sometimes the wall is where
we end up to begin letting go our llanto.

presence of [   ] / your absence made

SELF-PORTRAIT IN THE VA TELEMETRY WARD

where they are widening the narrow pathway

toward my father's heart and my uncle's passing

the time going on

about his time in the joint the time he spent

as a jail guard the time that Mexican

drug lord took a liking to him the time he offered him

a job on the outside as a bodyguard for his girl

about all the times he refused and how he'd never

wanted to spend his time working for anyone really

about how he knew it was time to quit the time

the inmates set a mattress on fire and he just *let the fucker burn*

how he knew it was time how he threw down his badge unhooked

his keys and *walked the fuck out* and how in the time before that

he'd learned the hard way to leave empty-handed the time

he'd left his father's house after he'd figured out how to steal

the family's fire and its secrets and how over time he came to be

bound by his father's liver-eating curse and all those times he used

to drink and let loose a buddy's secrets or steal his girl about that one time he hid a rifle in his coat and shot up a bar before

jumping into his buddy's idling van about all the time

he'd wasted and how in time he'd found himself

a more merciful God how now he spends his time trying

to make amends with his own sooted heart

how from time to time he will lie

on his thin mattress praying for a time

when his heart will break

open with the splintered light of the Sacred

Heart of Jesus radiating flame

crowned with thorns.

```
of [      ] / home
of [      ] / home
of [      ] / home
of [      ] / home
of [      ] / home
```

A HISTORY OF BAMBOO

The bamboo out back
is taking over—infantry

charging—steady invasion
from the neighboring city lot.

Each week another advance
nearer to the bedroom window

the view now only green
reed and yearning

stalk. *There is no stopping
the deep-running roots*

the garden guide instructs
unless a trench is dug

to uproot the system.
In Laos, a farmer digs

for bamboo shoots
and his spade strikes

a cluster bomb startled
from its mud-cradle.

At night the hollow poles rise
and answer to the wind.

Who knows how many
more will surface by morning.

If you notice next

HECUBA ON THE SHORES OF AL-FAW, 2003

Again the sea-machines creep from the east,
their Cronus jaws unlatched and pups expelled.
The scene the same. Again. Again. The sand
now boot-lace muck, the rutted shore resigned.
No words will do. Laments will not withstand
this thrashing tide. It's time for snarling beast-
speak. Gnash-rattle. Fracas-snap. Unmuzzled
hell-hound chorus unbound from roughened tongues.
Kynos-sema keen-keen lash-kaak nein grind
then ground and rot and reek and teeth and grief
and gabble ratchet growl: custodian
of woe. It doesn't end. Fleets on the reef,
horizon buckling. To meet what comes
the body cleaves from all that is human.

your [   ]
your [   ]
your [   ]

JUST A CLOSER WALK WITH THEE

1. 4 December 1969

> *The survivors, as we came to be known, of the December 4th raid . . . made a conscious decision not to participate in the grand jury investigation because we felt that we would get no justice through this investigation—that the intent of the grand jury was not to really see what was going on.*
>
> —Deborah Johnson (Akua Njeri) after the murder of Fred Hampton

Again a parade, star-spangled procession
of bullets obliterating blackness.

Blind light and ricochet—
then—nothing—
then—another round—

a fly-swarm circling the carcass:
he's good and dead now.

Deborah was a biblical warrior.

She said to remember:

There's only one thing
you have to print
in your story—

that's fascism—

do you know
how to spell it?

2. 4 December 2014

The fight isn't over—it's just begun.

—Esaw Garner, the day after the grand jury refused an indictment
for the murder of Eric Garner

How to spell it?

Do you know?

That's fascism.

In your story
you have to print,
there's only one thing
she said to remember:

Deborah was a biblical warrior.

He's good. And dead. Now,
a fly-swarm circling the carcass.

Then: another round.

Then: nothing.

Blind light and ricochet
of bullets obliterating blackness.

Again a parade, star-strangled procession.

the last of us.

YEAR OF THE DOG: AFTER-MATH, REPRISE

"2018 has been deadlier for schoolchildren than deployed service members"
—Washington Post

Some students crouch
under dorm room desks.
Some students are running away.
Some students stand still.
Some students are falling down.
Some students climb the stairs.
Some students are screaming.
Some students make no sound.
Some students stay inside.
Some students are bleeding out.
Some students bow their heads.
Some students are kneeling
over other students.
Some students are learning
new words to a song
they used to sing about the stars:
Lockdown, lockdown, Lock the door
Shut the lights off, Say no more
Go behind the desk and hide
Wait until it's safe inside
Lockdown, lockdown it's all done
Now it's time to have some fun!

she takes the staff

in her mouth,

and guides it

with her

stumps,

and writes

[text: Shakespeare, *Titus Andronicus*]

SELF-PORTRAIT IN THE TIME OF DISASTER

All morning my daughter pleading, *outside*
outside. By noon I kneel to button her
coat, tie' the scarf to keep her hood in place.
This is her first snow so she strains against
the ritual, spooked silent then whining,
restless under each buffeting layer,
uncertain how to settle into this
leashing. I manage at last to tunnel
her hands into mittens and she barks and
won't stop barking, her hands suddenly paws.
She's reduced to another state, barking
all day in these restraints. For days after
she howls into her hands, the only way
she knows now to tell me how she wants out.

108

my   mot

her   ' s   s

pang led

hand

i   work

POEM NOTES

"Lightening"
On 4 December 1969, Chicago Police murdered Black Panther leader, Fred Hampton, in his bed while he slept beside his pregnant fiancée, Deborah Johnson. Historical details about what Deborah Johnson endured and witnessed are drawn from: http:// digital.wustl.edu/e/eii/eiiweb/joh5427.0255.082marc_record_interviewee_process. html.

"Year of the Dog: Synonyms for Aperture"
On 4 May 1970, students gathered at Kent State University to protest the U.S. bombing of Cambodia. In response, the Ohio National Guard fired on the unarmed students, killing four and wounding nine others. The shooting led to subsequent campus protests, a nationwide student strike of nearly 4 million students, and hundreds of school closures across the country. John Filo, a Kent State student and part-time news photographer, captured the now iconic image of Mary Ann Vecchio kneeling and crying over the slain body of Kent State student, Jeffrey Miller. The photograph won the Pulitzer Prize in 1971 and has circulated widely as a symbol of student anti-war protest and the state violence mobilized and enacted against such actions. Quoted material from: https://iconicphotos.wordpress.com/2009/06/23/kent-state-shootings/, https://may4archive.org/ap_95.shtml, https://aadl.org/node/193128.

"Self-Portrait in Flesh and Stone"
Quoted material from: Gloria Anzaldúa, *Borderlands/La Frontera: The New Mestiza*, 4th Ed., 75; Yusef Komunyakaa, "Facing It," *Dien Cai Dau*, 63; Luke 19:40, New International Version; Sylvia Plath, "The Stones," *The Colossus and Other Poems*, 82.

"Year of the Dog: After-Math"
On 14 May 1970, ten days after the Kent State shooting, students at Jackson State College peaceably demonstrated against the war in Vietnam. The students were not armed. The National Guard and the city police descended on campus in response to the protest, and shortly after midnight on 15 May 1970 shot over 200 rounds within 28 seconds into Alexander Hall, a women's dormitory, leaving 2 students dead and 12 injured. Chronicle of the shooting taken from firsthand accounts recorded in the documentary video, *May 15, 1970: Gibbs/Green Tragedy at Jackson State University*.

"Edgewood Elegy"

Names of soldiers taken from the Edgewood memorial plaque at the Edgewood Veterans Stadium in San Antonio, TX.

Biographical details about soldiers, including dates of death, were drawn from http://www.vvmf.org/Wall-of-Faces, www.findagrave.com/memorials. Quoted material from: Wilfred Owen, "Dulce et Decorum Est," *Dulce et Decorum Est and Other Poems*; William Shakespeare, *Henry V*, "St. Crispin's Day Speech," (IV: iii, 18–67); my father's draft notice and naturalization papers.

"Self-Portrait in One Act"

As noted in the character descriptions, Everett Alvarez was the first American aviator POW captured in Vietnam. During his 8-year-long imprisonment, his sister, Delia Alvarez, became increasingly and publicly critical of the American involvement in Vietnam, defying state pressure to perform the long-suffering, patriotic POW family member. Instead, she regularly asserted a sense of racial, economic, and colonial affiliation between Chicanos and the Vietnamese people. Historical details about Delia and Everett Alvarez taken from: Mylene Moreno's documentary, *On Two Fronts: Latinos and Vietnam*; Everett Alvarez & Anthony Pitch's *Chained Eagle: The Heroic Story of the First American Shot Down over North Vietnam*; Natasha Zaretsky, "Private Suffering and Public Strife: Delia Alvarez's War with the Nixon Administration's POW Publicity Campaign, 1968–1973."

Dialogue not in italics takes poetic license. Dialogue in italics is quoted material from *On Two Fronts: Latinos and Vietnam*; "Private Suffering and Public Strife;" Marvin Gaye's songs, "What's Going On" & "What's Happening, Brother;" Stanley Kunitz, "The Testing-Tree;" Adrienne Rich, "The Break;" Lucille Clifton, "She Understands Me."

"Year of the Dog: A Rock and a Hard Place"

On 20 November 1969, nearly 80 Native Americans from numerous tribes calling themselves Indians of All Tribes reclaimed Alcatraz and occupied the island for 19 months. During their stay, they elected a governing council, issued the Alcatraz Proclamation and Letter, and invited the federal government to negotiate with them and to honor the previously broken treaties that reverted abandoned federal land to its original inhabitants. The original occupiers included LaNada Means (Shoshone Bannock) who emerged as a leader and spokesperson and John Trudell (Santee Sioux) who established and broadcasted "Radio Free Alcatraz." They were soon joined by others, garnered widespread media coverage, and exerted great influence on the eventual formation and actions of the American Indian Movement. Historical details taken from: Paul Chaat Smith & Robert Allen Warrior, *Like a Hurricane: The Indian Movement from Alactraz to Wounded Knee* and the documentary films, James Fortier's *Alcatraz Is Not an Island* and The National Park Service's *We Hold the Rock*. Song lyrics from Janis Joplin's version of "Summertime" and Buffy Sainte Marie's "Now that the Buffalo's Gone." John Trudell launched every broadcast of Radio Free Alcatraz with Buffy Sainte Marie's song. Quotes from Trudell's radio broadcasts are from https://www.juanpablopacheco.com/radio-free-alcatraz.

"Self-Portrait with Weeping Women"
Italicized phrase is taken from a speech by Hecuba in Euripides' *Trojan Women* (797–8).

"Year of the Dog: *Soledad*"
Angela Davis—intellectual, activist, prison abolitionist, and political prisoner— was captured by the FBI in New York City on 13 October 1970 and charged with murder, kidnapping, and conspiracy. She was detained at the New York Women's House of Detention (briefly in solitary confinement) and extradited to California on 22 December 1970. She stood trial from 28 February to 4 June 1972 and was eventually acquitted of all charges. She had been active in demanding the release of George Jackson and the other inmates at Soledad Prison who were wrongfully accused of murdering a white prison guard and who came to be known as the Sole- dad Brothers. Jackson's letters, written in prison, were published in his 1970 book, *Soledad Brother: The Prison Letters of George Jackson*. Historical details are drawn from: *Angela Davis: An Autobiography* and Shola Lynch's documentary, *Free Angela and All Political Prisoners*.

"Kim Phúc" Series of Poems in Section II
Phan Thi Kim Phúc survived the napalm attack, spending 14 months and under- going numerous surgeries at the Barsky Burn Unit in Saigon. She became a symbol for both the American antiwar movement and, after the war, for the Vietnamese communist regime's propaganda efforts. She studied in Cuba from 1986 until 1992, when she sought political asylum in Canada during a refueling stop on the way back from her honeymoon in Moscow. She now resides in Toronto where she founded the Kim Foundation International that provides aid to organizations that serve children affected by war.

Biographical details about Phan Thi Kim Phúc referenced in these poems are drawn from Denise Chong's *The Girl in the Picture: The Story of Kim Phuc, the Photograph, and the Vietnam War*.

Additional quotes from the following sources: "Kim Phúc in the Blast": "Hard bombs drop . . ." & "unwritten rule of engagement . . ." (Chong 63, 61); all other italicized passages are taken from testimony by Kim Phúc in "Girl Napalmed in Vietnam Says Past is Past, Forgives U.S.," *Montreal Gazette*, 20 August 1989: B1.

"Kim Phúc in the Photograph": Words attributed to Nick Ut and Kim Phúc are from the video "Napalm Girl" that was part of the exhibit, "The Vietnam War: 1945–1975," on display at the New York Historical Society from 4 Oct 2017–22 April 2018; Horst Faas quote is from "The Girl in the Photograph," *Los Angeles Times,* 20 Aug 1989: T8; headline and quote from General William Westmoreland is from "Viet War Photo is Challenged: Westmoreland Says Hibachi Not Napalm Burned Girl," *Washintgton Post*, 19 Jan 1986: A3; quote from Nhat Chi Mai, the Buddhist nun who set herself on fire as an act of protest against the Vietnam War, is documented in Trinh T. Minh-ha's documentary, *Surname Viet Given Name Nam* (1985).

"Self-Portrait with Howling Woman"
Italicized lyrics from the following Janis Joplin songs: "Maybe," "Cry Baby," "Try (Just a Little Bit Harder)," and "Kozmic Blues."

"*Surname Viet Given Name Nam*"
This poem is an ekphrastic response to Trinh T. Minh-ha's experimental, feminist documentary, *Surname Viet Given Name Nam* (1989) that chronicles the experiences of Vietnamese and Vietnamese-American women after the American War in Vietnam.

"Year of the Dog: Walls and Mirrors"
The italicized passages attributed to Maya Lin are drawn from an essay she wrote during the construction of the Vietnam Veterans Memorial in 1982 but did not publish until 2 November 2000 in "Making the Memorial," *The New York Review of Books.*

The reference to Antigone as an "in-between thing" is from Anne Carson's *Antigonick.*

It is important to note that the Vietnam Veterans Memorial Wall does not include the names of Vietnamese and South Asian refugees who continue to be affected by the war's legacy. The collective art/action project, "The Missing Piece Project" (missingpieceproject.org), is one among many endeavors that is intervening in this practice of memorial omission.

"A History of Bamboo"
Between 1964–1973, the U.S. military dropped 2 million tons of explosive ordnance

on Laos; 10–24 million cluster bombs or unexploded ordnances (UXOs) remain scattered across the country killing hundreds each year.

"Hecuba on the Shores of Al-Faw, 2003"
The U.S. invasion of Al-Faw in March 2003 was one of the first battles of the Iraq War (2003–2011).

"Just a Closer Walk with Thee"
Title taken from the traditional gospel hymn of the same name. This poem refers to the police murders of Fred Hampton (4 December 1969) and Eric Garner (17 July 2014) and to the grand jury decision (3 December 2014) to refuse indictment of Daniel Pantaleo, the officer who killed Garner, despite the medical examiner's report that ruled Garner's death a homicide. Epigraph quote and italicized passages in Part I are from Deborah Johnson's interview recorded for the documentary *Eyes on the Prize*. Full text archived at:
http://digital.wustl.edu/e/eii/eiiweb/joh5427.0255.082marc_record_interviewee_process.html
   Quote from Eric Garner's widow, Esaw Garner, is from:
https://www.usatoday.com/story/news/nation/2014/12/04/new-york-city-chokehold-eric-garner-protests-grand-jury/19881561/

"Year of the Dog: After-Math, Reprise"
The italicized text is an "active shooter drill" sung to the tune of "Twinkle Twinkle Little Star" that was taught to kindergarten students in Somerville, Massachusetts, in 2018.

IMAGE NOTES AND CREDITS

The Cover Design incorporates details from photographs taken by and of my father, Gilberto Villarreal, in Phu Bai in 1971 and details from Pierre Peyron's "Despair of Hecuba" (ca. 1784).

p14 "Rearview": Detail of snapshot my father took in Phu Bai, 1971.

p17 "Another shot, so you can imagine": Caption excerpts from my father's snapshots taken in Da Nang and Phu Bai, 1971.

p22 "Trying to speak, she barked": Text: Ovid, *Metamorphoses* 13: 568–569. Image: Detail of John Filo's photograph of Mary Ann Vecchio kneeling over the dead body of Jeffrey Miller, Kent State University, 4 May 1970. Filo/ Premium Archive/Getty Images.

p27 "Risen women looking out": Image: Jack Thornell's photograph of two unnamed female students looking out of a window frame in Alexander Dormitory, a women's residence hall at Jackson State College, following a police riot on 15 May 1970 that left 2 students dead and 12 injured, May 1970. Thornell/ AP.

p30 "Here is the entrance": Top: Caption excerpt from snapshot my father took near Phu Bai, 1971.
Bottom left: Detail of Horst Faas' photograph of a South Vietnamese woman covering her mouth as she stares into a mass grave near Dien Bai village where she fears the bodies of her missing husband, brother, and father may be buried, April 1969. Faas/AP
Bottom right: Detail of snapshot taken of my father extracting a tooth from a South Vietnamese boy, 1971.

p36 "Cross them to reach Da Nang": Top and Bottom: Detail of snapshot taken of my father, Phu Bai, 1971.
Middle: Caption excerpt from snapshot my father took near Da Nang, 1971.

p43 "Armature": Left and Right: Details of photos taken of my father in Phu Bai, 1971.

Middle: Detail of John Filo's photograph of Mary Ann Vecchio, Kent State University, 4 May 1970. Filo/Premium Archive/Getty Images.

p49 "Up in arms": Details of snapshots taken of my father in Da Nang and Phu Bai, 1971.

p52 "Here is another view": Top: Caption excerpts from snapshot my father took in Phu Bai, 1971.
Bottom: Detail from Otto Bettmann's photograph of students raising their fists in a Black Power salute following the memorial services for Phillip Lafayette Gibbs and James Earl Greene at Jackson State University, 21 May 1970. Bettmann/Bettmann Collection/Getty Images.

p57 Background Image: Nick Ut's photograph of Kim Phúc and her family running down Highway 1 in Tráng Bàng following a misdirected napalm attack by South Vietnamese forces on 8 June 1972. Ut/AP

p59 "The child in her birdgrief": Text: Anne Carson's translation of Sophokles, *Antigonick,* np.
Image: Detail of Nick Ut's photograph of Kim Phúc, 8 June 1972. Ut/AP

p62 "The highway is very narrow": Caption detail from snapshot my father took near Phu Bai, 1971.

p66 "Yelping griefbeast": Detail of snapshot my father took in Phu Bai, 1971.

p68 "Dark faces of the risen": Detail of snapshot my father took in Phu Bai, 1971.

p70 "Hence, I was trying": Text: Don Mee Choi, "6.25," *Hardly War,* 9.
Images: Caption details from snapshots my father took in Phu Bai and Da Nang, 1971.

p72 "Back/ground": Caption detail from snapshot my father took near Phu Bai, 1971.

p75 "Shornline": Detail of Nick Ut's photograph of Kim Phúc's napalm-burned arms, June 8, 1972. Ut/AP

p78 "Captured in the shot": Detail of my father holding his camera in his bunk in Phu Bai, 1971.

p83 "Here they are re-building" : Top: Detail of snapshot taken of my father and his Sanyo reel-to-reel, 1972.
Bottom: Details from Sal Veder's photograph of the reunion between former POW, Lt. Col. Robert L. Stirm, and his family, including his daughter Lorrie whose arms are pictured here, Travis Air Force Base, Fairfield CA, 17 March 1973. Veder/AP

p85 "So to speak": Text: Judges 5:12, New International Version.
Image: Caption excerpt from snapshot my father took in Phu Bai, 1971.

p89 "Keeps me": Top: Caption excerpt from snapshot my father took in Phu Bai, 1971.
Bottom: Details of snapshot taken of my father's hand in Phu Bai, 1971.

p91 "About half": Top: Detail of Sal Veder's photograph of Lorrie Stirm's arms, 17 March 1973. Veder/AP
Middle: Caption excerpt from snapshot my father took near Da Nang, 1971.
Bottom: Detail of snapshot taken of my father's arm in Phu Bai, 1971.

p94 "If you're looking for trouble": Left and right: Details of snapshot taken of my father reading the *Army Times* in Phu Bai, 1971.
Middle: Detail of snapshot I took of the Vietnam Veterans Memorial, circa 1983.

p99 "If you notice next": Top: Detail of Jack Thornell's photograph of two un-named female students looking out of a window frame in Alexander Dormitory, Jackson State College, May 1970. Thornell/AP
Bottom: Caption excerpt from snapshot my father took near Da Nang, 1971.

p104 "The last of us": Left: Detail from Otto Bettmann's photograph of students' Black Power salutes outside Alexander Dormitory, Jackson State College, 21 May 1970. Bettmann/Bettmann Collection/Getty Images.
Right: Caption excerpt from snapshot my father took near Da Nang, 1971.

p106 "She takes the staff": Text: William Shakespeare, *Titus Andronicus* IV:1.
Detail of Horst Faas' photograph of a mourning South Vietnamese woman near Dien Bai Village, April 1969. Faas/AP

ACKNOWLEDGMENTS

Grateful acknowledgements to the editors of the following publications in which versions of these poems first appeared:

Adanna Literary Journal: Special Issue on Women and War: "Lavinia Writing in the Sand, 1973," "Memorial Day Ghazal," "Last," and "Hecuba on the Shores of Da Nang" (current title: "Hecuba on the Shores of Al-Faw, 2003");

At Length: "Semi[idio][auto]matic" (serial poem that included: "A Show of Hands," "Armature," "Hearts and Minds," "Mother Tongue," and "Helen's About Face") and "Contact Sheet for Kim Phúc" (serial poem that included the poems in Section II: "Kim Phúc in the Temple of Cao Dai," "Kim Phúc in the Blast," "Kim Phúc in the Photograph," "Kim Phúc in the Barsky Burn Unit," "Kim Phúc in the Special Period," "Kim Phúc in the Temple of the Sun");

Boston Review: "Self-Portrait in Flesh and Stone";

Entre Guadalupe y Malinche: Tejanas in Literature and Art, eds. Ines Hernández Ávila and Norma E. Cantú, (Austin: University of Texas Press, 2016): "At the VA Telemetry Ward," (current title: "Self-Portrait in the VA Telemetry Ward");

Narrative Magazine: "After-Math," "Soledad," "Synonyms for Aperture" (current titles: "Year of the Dog: After-Math," "Year of the Dog: *Soledad*," "Year of the Dog: Synonyms for Aperture");

Pilgrimage Magazine: "A History of Bamboo";

Poem-A-Day: "Self Portrait with Weeping Women";

Poet Lore: "A Rock and a Hard Place" (current title: "Year of the Dog: A Rock and a Hard Place");

Poetry: "Wife's Disaster Manual," "Tía Lucia Enters the Nursing Home" (current title: "Self-Portrait in the Time of Disaster");

The Quarry: A Social Justice Poetry Database: "Walls and Mirrors, Fall 1982" (current title: "Year of the Dog: Walls and Mirrors");

RHINO Poetry Journal: "Lightening".

"A History of Bamboo," and "Lavinia Writing in the Sand, 1973" were reprinted in *Inheriting the War: Poetry and Prose by Descendants of Vietnam Veterans and Refugees* (Norton 2017).

"Wife's Disaster Manual" was featured in *Poetry Daily* (Sep 2012).

Thanks especially to the editors and judges of: *Poet Lore* for nominating "A Rock and A Hard Place" for a Pushcart Prize; *Split This Rock* for awarding "Walls and Mirrors, Fall 1982" 3rd Place in the Sonia Sanchez-Langston Hughes Poetry Contest; *RHINO Poetry Journal* for awarding "Lightening" Runner-Up for the RHINO Founders Prize.

I offer my sincerest appreciation to the BOA team for their support of and care with my work: Peter Conners, Ron Martin-Dent, Sandy Knight, Kelly Hatton, and Richard Foerster.

Thank you to Alexandra (allie) Taylor for their inspiring collaboration on cover art ideas and image logistics.

Melissa Montero at AP Images and Daniel Boland at Getty Images provided valuable assistance with acquiring photographic images and permissions.

Grateful acknowledgment to Columbia University's Office of the Executive Vice President of Arts and Sciences Division of Humanities' "War & Peace Initiative" Grant that supported the completion of this book.

Heartfelt gratitude to all those who inspired, supported, read, provided valuable feedback or research assistance on the poems in this book: Beca Alderete Baca, Amy Sayre Baptista, Julie Bathke, Marcellus Blount, Jody Bolz, Michelle Boyd, Cathy Linh Che, Juliana DeVaan, Nicole Dewey, Jonathan Farmer, Barbara Fischer, Sarah Gambito, Frank Guridy, Saidiya Hartman, Stefania Heim, Margo Jefferson, Daniel Alexander Jones, Yusef Komunyakaa, Marie Myung-Ok Lee, Celeste Guzmán Mendoza, Yesenia Montilla, Lisa L. Moore, Hoa Nguyen, Lien-Hang Nguyen, Viet Thanh Nguyen, Lisa Olstein, Hélène Quanquin, Samantha Pinto, Stacey Robinson, Clíona Ní Ríordáin, Carmen Giménez Smith, Susan Somers-Willett, Shirley Thompson, Natasha Trethewey, and Stacy Wolf.

Thanks especially to Aracelis Girmay for her advocacy as I searched for a home for this work.

Thanks as well to my wonderful poetry colleagues/comrades at Columbia: Timothy Donnelly, Dorothea Lasky, and Shane McCrae.

This book began to germinate during my residency at the Hedgebrook Center for Women Writers in August 2012. Special thanks to the Hedgebrook librarian, Evie Wilson Lingbloom, and to Anne Huggins who first suggested I write this book with and not just about my father. Thanks also to Rosa Rankin-Gee, Chauna Craig, Elizabeth Frost, Andrea Gunraj, Larissa Min, and Rafia Zakaria.

Abundant thanks to the sustaining communities of my CantoMundo *familia*, Kundiman (especially Sarah Gambito, Cathy Linh Che, and Joseph Legaspi), Cave Canem (especially Nicole Sealey), and the Poetry Coalition (especially Jennifer Benka).

Formal inspirations and models: Julie Bathke introduced me to Euripides' *Trojan Women* when I was 12 years old and set me on this path. I first encountered Trinh T. Minh-ha's *Surname Viet Given Name Nam* in the mid-1990s in a graduate seminar on Asian American Performance taught by James Moy. Its third world feminist ethos and experimental aesthetics indelibly shaped my approach to the topic of women and the "American War" in Vietnam. Recent works that have left their mark on mine: Don Mee Choi's *Hardly War*, Martha Collins's *Blue Front*, and Solmaz Sharif's *Look*. And always: Gwendolyn Brooks loitering in Mississippi.

I could not have conceived nor completed this book without the love and support of my family: my father, Gilberto Villarreal; my mother, Consuelo Villarreal; my Bronx parents, Francisco and Amparo Guridy; and my beloveds, Frank and Zaya Guridy.

ABOUT THE AUTHOR

Deborah Paredez is the author of a critical study, *Selenidad: Selena, Latinos, and the Performance of Memory* (Duke University Press), and of a poetry volume, *This Side of Skin* (Wings Press). She is the co-founder of CantoMundo, a national organization for Latinx poets, and a professor of creative writing and ethnic studies at Columbia University. She lives in New York City with her husband and daughter.

BOA EDITIONS, LTD.
AMERICAN POETS CONTINUUM SERIES

No. 1 *The Fuhrer Bunker: A Cycle of Poems in Progress*
W. D. Snodgrass

No. 2 *She*
M. L. Rosenthal

No. 3 *Living With Distance*
Ralph J. Mills, Jr.

No. 4 *Not Just Any Death*
Michael Waters

No. 5 *That Was Then: New and Selected Poems*
Isabella Gardner

No. 6 *Things That Happen Where There Aren't Any People*
William Stafford

No. 7 *The Bridge of Change: Poems 1974–1980*
John Logan

No. 8 *Signatures*
Joseph Stroud

No. 9 *People Live Here: Selected Poems 1949–1983*
Louis Simpson

No. 10 *Yin*
Carolyn Kizer

No. 11 *Duhamel: Ideas of Order in Little Canada*
Bill Tremblay

No. 12 *Seeing It Was So*
Anthony Piccione

No. 13 *Hyam Plutzik: The Collected Poems*

No. 14 *Good Woman: Poems and a Memoir 1969–1980*
Lucille Clifton

No. 15 *Next: New Poems*
Lucille Clifton

No. 16 *Roxa: Voices of the Culver Family*
William B. Patrick

No. 17 *John Logan: The Collected Poems*

No. 18 *Isabella Gardner: The Collected Poems*

No. 19 *The Sunken Lightship*
Peter Makuck

No. 20 *The City in Which I Love You*
Li-Young Lee

No. 21 *Quilting: Poems 1987–1990*
Lucille Clifton

No. 22 *John Logan: The Collected Fiction*

No. 23 *Shenandoah and Other Verse Plays*
Delmore Schwartz

No. 24 *Nobody Lives on Arthur Godfrey Boulevard*
Gerald Costanzo

No. 25 *The Book of Names: New and Selected Poems*
Barton Sutter

No. 26 *Each in His Season*
W. D. Snodgrass

No. 27 *Wordworks: Poems Selected and New*
Richard Kostelanetz

No. 28 *What We Carry*
Dorianne Laux

No. 29 *Red Suitcase*
Naomi Shihab Nye

No. 30 *Song*
Brigit Pegeen Kelly

No. 31 *The Fuehrer Bunker: The Complete Cycle*
W. D. Snodgrass

No. 32 *For the Kingdom*
Anthony Piccione

No. 33 *The Quicken Tree*
Bill Knott

No. 34 *These Upraised Hands*
William B. Patrick

No. 35 *Crazy Horse in Stillness*
William Heyen

No. 36 *Quick, Now, Always*
Mark Irwin

No. 37 *I Have Tasted the Apple*
Mary Crow

No. 38 *The Terrible Stories*
Lucille Clifton

COLOPHON

Blessing the Boats Selection titles spotlight poetry collections by women of color. The series is named in honor of Lucille Clifton (1936–2010) whose poetry collection *Blessing the Boats: New and Selected Poems 1988–2000* (BOA Editions), received the National Book Award. In 1988, Lucille Clifton became the first author to have two collections selected in the same year as finalists for the Pulitzer Prize: *Good Woman: Poems and a Memoir 1969–1980* (BOA), and *Next: New Poems* (BOA). Among her many other awards and accolades are the Ruth Lilly Poetry Prize, the Frost Medal, and an Emmy Award. In 2013, her posthumously published collection *The Collected Poems of Lucille Clifton 1965–2010* (BOA) was awarded the Hurston/Wright Legacy Award for Poetry.

◈

The publication of this book is made possible, in part, by the special support of the following individuals:

Anonymous
Angela Bonazinga & Catherine Lewis
Robert L. Giron
James Long Hale
Jack & Gail Langerak
Melanie & Ron Martin-Dent
Joe McElveney
Boo Poulin
Steven O. Russell & Phyllis Rifkin-Russell
William Waddell & Linda Rubel
Michael Waters & Mihaela Moscaliuc